Go Fast, Turn Left:
Simple Instructions for Following Jesus

By

Joseph McRae Mellichamp

LEWIS AND STANLEY
4901 Keller Springs Road, Suite 106
Addison, TX 75001-0129

Scripture references are taken from the NEW AMERICAN STANDARD BIBLE®, Copyright © 1960, 1962, 1968, 1971, 1973, 1975, 1977, 1995, by the Lockman Foundation. Used by permission.

Note: Additional copies of *Go Fast, Turn Left* can be purchased online at: http://clmstore.stores.yahoo.net

ISBN: 1-4276-0200-X

Printed in the United States of America

To Jonathan and Jennifer.
"I have no greater joy than this, to hear of my children walking in the truth." 3 John 4

GO FAST, TURN LEFT:
Simple Instructions for Following Jesus

Contents

GO FAST, TURN LEFT
Introduction

Go Fast, Turn Left. What a strange title for a book. What does it mean? I'll tell you on the next few pages, and then you will understand. But first, I need to tell you how the book came to be written and what the book is about.

I lead a Bible study called *Daybreak for Men* in the area of Atlanta, Georgia, where I live. Every Friday morning from 6:30 to 8:30, 40-50 men gather together to gulp down donuts and coffee, to banter with each other, and to consider the Bible and how to apply it to our lives. A year or so ago we started to study Rick Warren's wonderful book, *The Purpose Driven Life* [Rick Warren, *The Purpose Driven Life*, Grand Rapids, MI: Zondervan, 2002]. We take a chapter a week, with a forty minute lecture on the chapter for the group and then we divide into small groups to discuss how the material applies to our lives as husbands, fathers, businessmen, and followers of Jesus.

Several months ago, we covered Day 37. The topic title for that day was "Sharing Your Life Message." In the text, Warren writes that we all have a life message to share and that it consists of four parts: our testimony, our life lessons, our Godly passions, and the Good News. He defines life lessons as the most important lessons God has taught us.

As I was preparing to teach the lesson, I reflected over my life and made a list of the five most important things God has taught me in my nearly fifty years of following Him. After sharing these with about 45 guys who came that Friday morning, I thought, "Why would I share important truths I have learned with a bunch of guys at *Daybreak for Men* and not share them with my family for their benefit?" And one of the guys that morning even suggested that I send my life lessons in a letter to my family.

So I determined to write my life lessons down and flesh them out so I could send them over the next few weeks to our two adult children who live in another state. In the lecture that Friday, I only had time to mention each of the five life lessons briefly. I have since developed each of the ideas in detail along with some application questions. As I started sending them one at a time to our children I wrote, "I don't know what you will do with these lessons. I hope you will read them and consider them and take them to heart. Maybe you can file them away and when I am no longer

1

around, you'll at least have a good idea of what was important to me. So here goes. Life Lesson Number 1 is attached. Love, Dad."

And about half way through the process of fleshing out these five lessons, I began to be impressed that I ought to share them with a wider audience, because, in my experience, most of us struggle with these same issues. I believe the things the Lord has taught me over many years of walking with Him, will also be helpful to you no matter where you are in your journey with Him. So here goes. Life Lesson Number 1 follows. Love, Rae Mellichamp.

GO FAST, TURN LEFT
Priorities

Believe it or not, one of the most significant things I have learned as a Christian came from an outdoor billboard advertisement for beer. That's right—beer. At least, I think it was a beer advertisement. Let me explain. I was driving into Atlanta one day several years ago from our home in the suburbs, and I recall absently noticing the message on a billboard by the roadside. The ad featured a racecar driver whom I later determined to be Rusty Wallace. Rusty had his helmet tucked under his arm and was leaning on his racecar. The caption on the ad as I recollect read as follows:

Rusty's Do List:

1. Go fast.
2. Turn left.

I suspect there was other text on the ad, but I either didn't have time to process it or quickly forgot it. It took a few seconds for the logic of Rusty's Do List to sink in. Although I am not a racing fan and know virtually nothing about the sport, driving a racecar around a 2 mile track at speeds in excess of 200 miles an hour must be an incredibly complex undertaking. In a 500 mile race, a racecar driver would have to make thousands of decisions—any one of which could mean life or death. To be able to reduce auto-racing in all of its complexity to its bare essentials—*Go Fast, Turn Left*—is a remarkable thing, even if only for a beer advertisement.

As I turned this clever wording over and over in my mind, I thought, "What a wonderful metaphor of the Christian life this is!" For the follower of Jesus, all of life can be summed up in a simple Do List.

Joe Believer's Do List:

1. Seek Jesus.
2. Everything else.

The most important activity in the life of a believer is to learn of Jesus, to get to know Him, to cultivate a personal relationship with Him. Everything else is a distant second to the opportunity we have to seek Him and to know Him.

Over and over in the New Testament, we see Jesus reinforcing this idea. We see it in the wonderful story of the dinner at the home of Lazarus and his sisters Mary and Martha in Bethany described in Luke 10:38-42. Luke tells us that Mary "was listening to the Lord's word, seated at His feet. But Martha was distracted with all her preparations; and she came up to Him and said, 'Lord, do You not care that my sister has left me to do all the serving alone? Then tell her to help me.'" Jesus' response here has profound implications for His followers, yet, I suspect that the vast majority of people who read this narrative, miss the point. He replies, "Martha, Martha, you are worried and bothered about so many things; but only a few things are necessary, really only one, for Mary has chosen the good part, which shall not be taken away from her." What is Jesus really saying here?

The fact that Jesus called Martha's name twice indicates that He is trying to break through her distraction, to get her to remove herself from her present circumstances, and to focus on what He is going to say to her next. Then He states this absolutely remarkable principle, "There is really only one thing necessary in life—to know Me, to hear My word, to be in My presence. Mary has discovered this. You, on the other hand, are occupied with things which in comparison to being in My presence are trivial. Oh, they may be important things. They may be necessary things. They may be crucial things. But compared to being with Me, they are trivial. I am not going to tell Mary to stop doing the only truly necessary thing in life— spending time in My presence—to do something else that, while it may seem important to you, is in the grand scheme of things really trivial."

And isn't this the way we live our lives? We are distracted by the trivial minutiae of life to the extent that we fail to seek Him. Our schedules are packed from morning to night with the busyness of life. Oh, they are important things. Making a living. Raising a family. Fighting a war. Getting an education. Teaching a Sunday School Class. Reading a book. Taking a trip. These are usually important things. These are often necessary things. But compared to being with Jesus these things, no matter how necessary or important they may actually be, are all trivial.

In the Sermon on the Mount, Jesus told His disciples, "But seek first His Kingdom and His Righteousness; and all these things shall be added to you (Matthew 6:33)." The context of the passage is Jesus speaking to a large crowd (and to us today) about the important concerns of life—food, and drink, and clothing—necessary things. And His conclusion is to inform us that our heavenly Father knows our needs and that He will provide these things for us in abundance—if we will only seek Him as the first priority of our lives.

In other words, God knows about my job situation, He knows about my family problems. He knows about my health issues. He knows I am lonely. He knows I have relational issues with family members, neighbors, and friends. He knows all of this. And He assures me, that if I will just seek Him as the priority of my life, He will take care of all the other things in His time and in His way. This is the best deal in the history of mankind. Think of it. If I seek Him with all of my heart, He obligates Himself to take care of every other detail of my life. Now this doesn't mean that I can take a pass on all of these things. Of course, I still need to do my best, to work hard, to be diligent, to take risks, to set ambitious goals. But I can do these things knowing that my heavenly Father has my best interests at heart and that He will accomplish the things which concern me. Why wouldn't I agree to these terms?

The Westminster Catechism puts it another way. "The chief end [purpose] of man is to glorify God and enjoy Him forever." What does this really mean? *Go Fast, Turn Left.* The primary purpose of my life is to know God, to worship Him, to enjoy Him. Everything else is icing on the cake of life. If I succeed in fulfilling my primary purpose, I succeed, regardless of whatever else I might accomplish. Oh, there is much more to be sure. God has a plan for each of us and the great joy of life is experienced in discovering His plan for us. But, if I fail in my primary purpose, I fail, regardless of how spectacularly I might succeed in every other area. Jesus said in Mark 8:36, "What does it profit a man if he gains the whole world and loses his soul?" I may become CEO of a Fortune 500 company, win an Olympic gold medal, command an army, become a famous Hollywood star—whatever, you name it; if I don't have a rich relationship with God, the rest is worthless. This is exactly the point of the parable of the rich fool in Luke 12:16-21.

In Matthew 22:37,38, Jesus frames the argument another way. "You shall love the Lord your God with all your heart, and with all your soul and with all your mind. This is the great and foremost commandment." I can only begin to love God as I should if I am willing to put everything else in life after Him; if I am willing to seek Him as the most important activity of my life. My Do List has to read: "1. Seek Jesus, 2. Everything else." To have it any other way is to disobey what in the mind of Jesus was the most important commandment. If my family, or my job, or my health, or anything else becomes so prominent in my life that it causes

5

my focus on Jesus to take second place in my attention, I have broken the commandment.

What is a person to do when he or she begins to realize this truth? I can tell you how it affected me. When these ideas began to take root in my mind, I knew I had to make a decision. I knew that to really seek Jesus above all else in my life, at the very minimum, I needed to be willing to seek Him as *the most important* activity of my life. In a very practical way, I determined that I would spend time with Him listening to His word as the most important activity in my life every day for the rest of my life. What could possibly be more important than spending time "listening to Lord's word, seated at His feet?" No matter how I protest, if I put other things before spending time with Him, I don't value Him as I ought. I am allowing other things to take the place of prominence in my life that He desires.

Now, exactly how does one seek Jesus as the most important activity of his or her life? That is the topic of my second life lesson. For now, let me close this lesson by reiterating that one of the most significant things I have learned came from a beer advertisement. *Go Fast, Turn Left.* If you can come to grips with this, you really have gained a profound understanding of the way Jesus wants us to order our priorities—seek Him first, everything else second. Here are a couple of questions for you to mull over:

Questions

1. What does the Do List of your life look like? Does seeking Jesus even appear on the list? Does it make the top ten activities?

2. Do you agree that compared to spending time with Jesus, everything else in life comes in a very distant second? Why do you suppose it is so difficult to live as though this is so?

3. What would it take for you to rearrange your priorities so that they become: (1.) Seek Jesus, (2.) Everything else?

4. Jesus said, "You shall love the Lord your God with all your heart, and with all your soul and with all your mind. This is the great and foremost commandment." Do you understand that following this command might require you to radically rearrange your priorities?

6

Explain how this would be so.

5. How do you think your life would be different if you were to actually begin to live in obedience to this principle?

GO FAST, TURN LEFT
Time

If the most significant lesson I have learned as a Christian came from a beer advertisement, the second most significant lesson came from watching football games on television. What do I mean? In the last chapter, I suggested that, for the Christian, the most important thing and, indeed, the only necessary thing, is to seek Jesus, to put Him above everything else in life. But how does one do that? To seek Jesus and to put Him first in one's life is certainly a worthwhile intention; indeed, it is God's admonition for all believers. But intentions don't just come to pass by accident. How do intentions become reality? How does one translate a general statement of intention or aspiration into very specific steps which one can accomplish to ensure that the intention is realized? Well, the answer to this important question, as it relates to putting Jesus first in my life, I have found is in the way I use my time.

In order to put Jesus first in my life, I need, at a minimum, to be willing to spend time with Him. If you think about it, the most important thing in the life of a Christian after coming to Christ is spending time in the Scripture and in prayer seeking to know God and seeking His will. This single thing is one of the keys to spiritual maturity—there are no shortcuts. One can't take a pill. One can't have an experience. And God certainly is not going to wave a wand over us and transform us magically into mature believers in the twinkling of an eye. It is only as we are consistently in the Word, applying it to our lives and discussing it with our heavenly Father, that we begin to grow up as believers.

The Apostle Paul asked two questions when he encountered the living Lord on the road to Damascus (Acts 22:8,10). "Who are You, Lord?" and "What shall I do, Lord?" For the Christian, these questions are of primary importance. Taken in a general sense, the first expresses the importance of knowing God and the second the necessity of discovering His will for our life. The believer who is seeking answers to these questions on a daily basis will be experiencing a dynamic personal relationship with Christ, and moving toward maturity as a disciple. Paul later underscored the importance of the devotional life for the believer, "so faith comes from hearing and hearing by the word of Christ (Romans 10:17)." I am personally satisfied that one's devotional life is a fairly good barometer of how earnestly he or she is seeking Jesus, of the prominence Jesus occupies in his or her life. If I never spend time with Jesus, how can I possibly say that He is important to me? On the other hand, if I am consistently spending time with Jesus in His word and in prayer as the priority of my life, it is almost certain that He will become more and more the central focus of my life, the most important thing in my life.

But there is a huge problem here. Everyone I know and everyone you know is *slammed*—as the expression goes. We are all overwhelmed with things to do. There is never enough time to do all the things that clamor for our attention. How can I seek Jesus, how can I put Him first in my life if I am already maxed out on the time I have available? Even if you agree that seeking Him is to be the most important thing in your life, how do you accomplish this in the midst of the busyness of life? I am convinced that the single most difficult issue that Christians living in the 21st century grapple with is having a consistent devotional life. For many years, I have questioned people about their devotional lives, and ninety plus percent of them are either struggling with this issue or have given up on it altogether. I have been involved with laymen as a teacher and church leader for many years, and I know of very few believers, men or women, who are succeeding in this important area. This is really quite remarkable!

So if the devotional life is of such vital importance in the life of the believer, why are so few believers experiencing success in this area of their lives? Here are a few revelations I have had as I have come to terms with this issue. In the late 1970s, I can't recall the exact date, my wife Peggy and I enrolled in a discipleship program at our church. This particular program was developed by the Navigators, a ministry that is known for discipleship. As we embarked on the program, we learned that there were requirements that we would be responsible for completing and signing off on every week. Things like memorizing Scripture verses (another thing the Navigators are known for), writing our personal testimony (which we had already done), and a number of other very good and profitable things. The big deal, though, which everyone quickly figured out, was to have a "Quiet Time" (a devotional from the Scripture which we would record in a notebook) every day for 14 consecutive days. For everyone in our group, this was a challenge equivalent to standing at the foot of Mount Everest and thinking about reaching the summit

For everyone but me, that is. I had been having devotions for some years and had been recording the things God had been teaching me in a notebook. Now, I am a box-checker. I get great satisfaction from checking off things on my Do List; and I was eagerly looking forward to being the first in our group to scale the mountain. So much so, that I decided just to do it retroactively. Here was the plan. I would go to my devotional notebook and look backward through my notes until I found 14 days in a row and then check the box. No need to wait for 14 new days to pass. Wow, was I in for a shock! I turned pages and turned pages. I went all the way to the beginning of my devotional notes—and I couldn't find 14 consecutive days! I would go for a week and then I would miss a day; or I would have four or five devotions in a row and then would miss five or six. After reviewing my entire written devotional history, the only conclusion I could reach was that I wasn't very consistent in my devotional life!

So I dutifully started like the others in our class and did my 14 days in a row, and then kept going. Eventually I missed a day. I started over. But pretty soon I was back in the same old rut of five or six days on, a couple of days off—you know the drill. The idea behind the discipleship program was that having devotions would become a habit, something that we automatically did, like eating, or sleeping. The problem, you see, is that we live such hectic lives, filled with so much activity, that some days it is just impossible to set aside time to spend in God's word. Or so I thought. And it is pretty easy to rationalize. I was a busy professor with teaching and research obligations, I had a family to provide for and take care of, and church and neighborhood obligations to accomplish. And besides, no one else I knew was succeeding in this area, so why did I think I might be different? So the years passed. I can only characterize my devotional life during that period as luke-warm. Then came a lesson from television football.

I was sitting in my lounge chair watching Monday Night Football one night when, in a moment of distraction, I started thinking about my devotional life. And I started to rationalize as I had done often in the past. I'm really too busy with the activities of life to have regular devotion times. Then it occurred to me what I was doing. I had time each Monday night to watch Monday Night Football. I watched a college game or two on Saturdays and a professional game on Sunday afternoon. I was really happy when they started doing Thursday Night Football so I could catch another college game on Thursday. Here I was watching a minimum of 15 to 20 hours of football a week and simultaneously claiming that I was too busy to spend a few minutes each day with the Creator of the universe in His word and in conversation with Him.

I was forced by the sheer incongruity of my rationalization to admit that my arguments just didn't cut it. On reflection, I had to conclude that I find time to do the things that are really important to me. As a friend

11

of mine puts it, "We do what we want to do." Furthermore, I understood the flip side of the proposition: if I habitually neglect something in my life, there is a very good reason—it isn't that important. That's right. No matter how much I protest, if I look at my calendar, I can pretty much tell what is important to me. I find time to do what is important, so my calendar is a pretty accurate reflection of my priorities. If I have time for my work, for sports activities, for travel, for family, but no time for God, I have to conclude that these activities are all more important to me than spending time with the Lord.

This is pretty powerful logic. But it is true. It stung to think this way. What was I communicating to the Lord when I spent hours each week glued to the television watching ball games and consistently neglecting my relationship with Him? "Lord, I'm really sorry, but football is 20 times more important to me than You are!" Ridiculous! But this is the only conclusion I could draw. So what does one do when faced with this state of affairs? I determined that if I am really serious about my relationship with God, spending time with Him must be THE most important activity of my day. It should preempt everything else—eating, sleeping, working, everything. So I have adopted this as the guiding principle for allocating my time—I intend to spend time each day, every day for the rest of my life seeking God through His word and in prayer as THE priority of my life.

Now I reached these conclusions years ago and I can honestly say I have constantly lived with this as my intention. That doesn't mean I always have my devotions before I do anything else. But it has meant that I consistently spend time with Him. It takes some personal activity scheduling to accomplish this, but it can be done. Some days, I have my devotional time before I do anything else; some days it is the last thing I do before retiring. But early every day, I plan when I will set aside time to spend with the Lord that day and then I do it. So if you looked at my devotional notebook for the last decade, you would conclude that spending time with God is high on my agenda. And, based on consistency alone, you would conclude that it is at the top of the list. And this is really the important thing, we are not attempting to earn medals for consecutive devotionals, we want to be consistently seeking Jesus through His word.

Because the devotional life is so vital in the walk of a believer and because, in my experience, so few believers are succeeding in this area, I am including in Appendix 1 a brief article I wrote over twenty years ago that describes a simple devotional approach. I have been using this method for twenty-five or more years and I have consistently enjoyed rich times of fellowship with God through His Word. If you are one of those who is struggling in this regard, take a look at this material and try the approach for a few days; I expect that it will help you begin to experience some exciting times with the Lord. Once you begin to develop some effective and consistent devotional practices, and not before, I want to commend one other discipline related to reading Scripture for your consideration. Have you ever read the Bible through from cover to cover? I don't know if there are any statistics available on the number of believers who might have successfully accomplished this challenge—my suspect is that very few, especially lay people, have done so. In Appendix 2, I am including a brief challenge to accomplish this along with some helpful material on how. Now let's continue our discussion on managing our time.

Once one has determined that the devotional time is of utmost importance and has begun to make it the first priority each day, then it is helpful to begin to look at the whole issue of time management. We don't have time or space in this little volume on Life Lessons to probe very deeply into this topic, but I can at least point you in the direction of some material that has been extremely helpful to me over the years and perhaps give you some quick tips that will help as you begin to focus on managing your time more effectively. The two authors who have been most helpful to me in this regard are Charles Hummel and Stephen Covey. Hummel published a little brochure called *The Tyranny of the Urgent* in 1967 that identifies the main challenge most people face in managing their lives— they have trouble discriminating between importance and urgency [Charles E. Hummel, *Tyranny of the Urgent*, Downers Grove, IL: InterVarsity Press, 1967]. In his two best-selling books, *The Seven Habits of Highly Effective People* and *First Things First*, Covey lays out a very good process for classifying activities on the basis of these two attributes— importance and urgency—and then allocating time to accomplish important activities [Stephen R. Covey, *The Seven Habits of Highly Effective People*, New York: Simon and Schuster, 1989], [Covey, Stephen R., A. Roger Merrill, and Rebecca R. Merrill, *First Things First*, New York: Simon and Schuster, 1994].

Let me give you a *Cliff Notes* summary that will help you get started until you can do some additional reading along these lines. First, identify the different areas of focus of your life—for most people these will be things like: relationships (God, spouse, children, parents, etc.), job, church, recreation/hobbies, finances, physical life, and so forth. We call these areas *roles*. Now, for each important role area, decide what you would like to accomplish or become over the next months and years of your

13

life. We call these aspirations *life goals*. Then take a few moments each week and identify for each role one or two things you could do that week to help you accomplish your life goal for that role. These activities are called *weekly goals*. You have just identified the most important things you could possibly accomplish during the coming week. These are your *first things*! Finally, remember Covey's book title *First Things First*; ensure each week that you schedule time to work on your first things. And whatever you do, as you begin to implement these ideas, don't let the urgent things prevent you from doing the important things. I have been following this process hard since the early 1990s and I can tell you that it will pay major dividends. Give it a shot—I think you will benefit from the effort.

Before we wrap up this lesson on the issue of time, I want us to consider one other aspect of our use of our time. The fourth of the Ten Commandments deals exclusively with the issue of time. It says, "Remember the Sabbath day, to keep it holy (Exodus 20:8)." For most of my Christian life, I half-heartedly tried to observe the Sabbath—to set aside Sunday as a day of rest. I made sure my family was in church on Sunday and avoided stuff like yard work and **work** work and shopping unless unavoidable. But I have to admit that until a few years ago, I really didn't have a great appreciation for the real meaning of the Sabbath. That all changed on reading A. B. Bruce's great Christian classic, *The Training of the Twelve* [Alexander Balmain Bruce, *The Training of the Twelve*, Grand Rapids, MI: Kregel Publications, 1988]. Bruce, a Scottish clergyman writing in 1871 said of the Sabbath, "It was not a day taken from man by God with a demanding spirit, but a day given by God in mercy to man—God's holiday to His subjects. ... The best way to observe the Sabbath is that which is most conducive to man's physical and spiritual well-being—in other words, that which will be best for his body and soul. In the light of this principle, you will keep the holy day in a spirit of intelligent joy and thankfulness to God the Creator for His gracious consideration toward His creatures." Think of it, God has given us this wonderful holiday—more than a tenth of each week—one day out of seven; a day to rest and to worship Him. What an incredible gift. How could I not receive this gift and all it entails with joy and thankfulness?

Sometime after reading Bruce's recommendation for observing the Sabbath, I read in *The New Living Translation* of the Bible what God Himself has to say about His gift to us. It changed my attitude forever. "Keep the Sabbath day holy. Don't pursue your own interests on that day, but enjoy the Sabbath and speak of it with delight as the Lord's holy day. Honor the Lord in everything you do, and don't follow your own desires or

talk idly. If you do this, the Lord will be your delight. (Isaiah 58:13-14a)."
I try to slip out of bed onto my knees every Sunday morning to thank God
for His gift of the Sabbath and to read Isaiah 58:13-14a every Sunday
morning as I am settling into my seat in church just to remind myself of the
incredible gift God has given us in His Sabbath. What a loving God He is!
Who wouldn't want to spend time with Him, to worship Him and to know
him?

Let me offer a story that will highlight some of the possibilities
that are in the offing when we start managing our time based on Biblical
priorities. When I first started teaching at the University of Alabama in the
early 1970s, I became involved as faculty advisor to the local chapter of my
college social fraternity. In that connection, I became acquainted with Dr.
Raymond McLain, who was one of the most interesting men I have ever
had the pleasure of knowing. Dr. McLain had been president of
Transylvania University in Kentucky and also of the American University
in Cairo, Egypt. When I knew him, he was Academic Vice President of the
University of Alabama and, therefore, my boss several levels removed. He
was also the district chief or regional director of the fraternity in charge of
chapters in Alabama, Mississippi, and Louisiana. Mrs. McLain was
director of the university's institute of Southern folklore and culture. They
were both fascinating people—very cultured and refined. The McLain's
home resembled a museum of Middle Eastern artifacts; their son and
grandchildren performed as a Bluegrass band of some renown and their
daughter wrote Bluegrass music.

Dr. McLain obviously took a liking to me and apparently imagined
himself as a mentor to me. We were occasionally invited to their home and
I spent many enjoyable hours in his office—every time he spoke it was a
lesson, in history, or world politics, or culture. He taught a short course in
woodcuts and offset printing which I took and thoroughly enjoyed—we still
treasure some of the pieces I completed under his watchful eye. One day,
he made me a fantastic offer. "Rae," he said, "why don't you take over my
job as district chief of the fraternity? I'll teach you the job. We'll drive
down to Tulane University in New Orleans and I'll introduce you to the
president of Tulane who is a personal friend. We'll go over to the
University of Mississippi and Mississippi State University and I'll introduce
you to the presidents there, both of whom are personal friends." In other
words he was saying, "I will connect you with the powerful academic
figures in the Southeast; you will have a network in academia that would be
the envy of every young professor in the region." What a deal!

At the time, Peggy and I had been challenged to join the staff of Campus Crusade for Christ as associate (or part-time) staff with the faculty ministry. In this connection, we would be investing several hours each week in ministry with students and other Christian professors and we would be required to do a two-week training assignment every summer. There would also be some travel in this involvement with Crusade. As a young, untenured assistant professor with a wife and two young children who was trying to get established in the university, either one of these opportunities—district chief of the fraternity or associate staff of Crusade—would have been a stretch; to take on both would have been out of the question. So I had a very clear choice. Either accept what would have surely been a fast track to success in academe or follow what I thought at the time was God's leading and affiliate with Crusade. I had to make a choice—I couldn't do both.

Well, it really was no decision. I told Dr. McLain that we had decided to affiliate with Campus Crusade for Christ as part of the faculty ministry and that I would not be able to continue with my fraternity activities. He was disappointed; I heard as much through acquaintances later. But that has been the only down-side of that decision. I went on to have an absolutely fantastic career in the university. I taught and did research in a fascinating high tech area, my research received national and international recognition, I consulted with some of the most prestigious companies and government agencies in the country, and I was able to have an impact for Jesus in the lives of many of my students. What about our connection with Campus Crusade for Christ? Today we are in the 36th year of that association with Christian Leadership Ministries, the faculty ministry of Campus Crusade. Discovering how to restore Christian truth to the universities of the world has been my absolute passion since the very first day—it is what I eat, sleep, and breathe on a daily basis. In this ministry Peggy and I have spoken on some 200 university and college campuses in this country and a dozen countries abroad. We were able to minister as a couple together through all of my time as a professor and now well into our retirement years. In fact, I can't imagine myself ever doing anything else. In short, that decision became the defining moment of my life—it presented me with the challenge of a lifetime. When Jesus said in Matthew 6:33, "But seek first His kingdom and His righteousness, and all these things will be added to you," He wasn't making empty promises to make us feel good, He was obligating Himself to honor our small commitments to put Him in His rightful place in our lives.

Well, this discussion of managing time started a few pages ago with me in front of a television set. So you see, watching television *can* be beneficial. But only if you think about other things in the background. And just for the record, I rarely ever watch sports programs on television anymore—I have better things to do.

Questions

1. Do you agree that, for the Christian, seeking God and His will through His word and in prayer is the most important activity of life?

2. What is your devotional life like? If it is like that of most Christians, do you take comfort in knowing that you are really not so different from the next person?

3. If we were to examine your calendar for the last several months, what would we likely conclude is really important to you? Would seeking the Lord in His word and through prayer even appear on your radar screen?

4. What would it take for you to determine that THE most important activity every day for the rest of your life is to seek God through His word and prayer?

5. What would it take for you to identify for each major area of your life your first things and to begin to accomplish them on a consistent basis?

GO FAST, TURN LEFT
Money

I am convinced that the single most misunderstood aspect of the Christian life has to do with stewardship or, in simple terms, with how we manage money. Ask just about any individual who does not attend church on a regular basis why they don't and he or she is very likely to respond by saying something like, "All the church is interested in is my money." And even those who are church members and attend regularly often don't understand Biblical concepts of stewardship. Studies show that only about four percent of Americans gave ten percent of their income to churches in 2004; among "born again" Christians [people who are likely to say their faith really matters] the numbers are only modestly better, about nine percent of them tithe.

A number of reasons are cited for this phenomenon—from "churches aren't able to effectively communicate need" to "people are just plain selfish." From my own experience, I think the fundamental reason people, and especially Christians, handle money with a tight fist is because they just don't understand money from God's perspective. So let me share some of the things I have picked up along the way with regard to managing financial resources God's way; we'll call this *Money 101*. Certainly, the beginning point in this has to be an understanding of who God is and who we are.

John Piper clearly identified the key issue when he wrote, "God has no needs that I [or anyone else] could ever be required to satisfy, God has no deficiencies that I might be required to supply. He is complete in himself." [John Piper, *The Pleasures of God: Meditations on God's Delight in Being God*, Portland, OR: Multnomah, 1991, pp. 215-216] Or as the Bible puts it, "For every beast of the forest is Mine, the cattle on a thousand hills. I know every bird of the mountains, and everything that moves in the field is Mine. If I were hungry I would not tell you, for the world is Mine, and all it contains." Psalm 50:10-12 How utterly arrogant of us to think that God needs money, or anything else for that matter. In writing this, I have studiously refrained from using the term "our money." It is not our money! God owns everything as the Scriptures remind us. We own nothing. We are stewards of God's possessions. God has entrusted some of His resources to us to manage for Him. We desperately need to learn from Him how to manage our financial (and other) resources.

I first began to suspect that God operates in this realm a whole lot differently than we do shortly after I started to really get serious about my commitment to Christ. In the summer of 1970, Peggy and I were invited to attend a "Congress of Christian Faculty" to be held at Campus Crusade for Christ's headquarters at Arrowhead Springs, California. This was the first such conference of its kind and as a new university professor and a relatively new Christian I figured that it would be an important event for me to attend. The contacts in the Christian academic community I would make and relationships with Christian professors I would form could not easily be made in any other venue. But, there was one very large problem—money. Campus Crusade had generously offered to underwrite the meals and lodging for all conference participants, but we would be required to cover our travel and other incidental expenses. At the time I was making about $13,000 a year, we were living in a rented house with early attic and early basement furnishings, and sharing one automobile among the four of us. Peggy and I were saving every dime we could scrape up for a second car. We probably had $300 in savings—I forget the exact details. Whatever it was, it was enough to cover our airfare to California and any other expenses we were likely to incur on the trip.

So we had a very clear choice. We could continue to stash away money for another vehicle (and we were within striking distance of our target) or we could withdraw our savings and attend the conference, postponing the automobile purchase for another year or so. After talking it over, we decided that this conference was important enough for discerning God's plan for our life in academia, that it warranted any sacrifice on our part. The car could wait, we would somehow manage without it. So we went to California, and the conference was everything we hoped it might be and a whole lot more. We became lifelong friends with Walter and Ann Bradley; at the time Walter was a young professor at the Colorado School of Mines and Ann was a homemaker and mom like Peggy. For the past thirty-five years we have labored together as university professors ministering in the name of Christ in the universities of the world. Walter and others at the conference challenged me for the first time to try to understand what it means to be a Christian professor in the university and how to represent Christ through my teaching and research. As I mentioned earlier, this has been my life's passion, nothing before or since has gripped my imagination so thoroughly.

After the conference we returned to the University of Alabama. Back from the mountaintop to face the realities of life—one of which was we were an active family of four with one set of wheels. But not for long.

Shortly after school started in September, Peggy's younger brother Barry called to ask a favor. The previous summer he had purchased a new Volkswagen camper—complete with a pop-up roof—and he had just received orders to go to Vietnam in the U.S. Army. He didn't want (or couldn't bring himself) to part with his camper. Would we be willing to keep it for him and drive it for the year he was to be overseas? Would we? Would we? We most assuredly would! So we inherited an almost new Volkswagen camper for the year. During the year we took a trip to the outer banks of North Carolina, camping all the way, of course. And we did a grand tour of Florida in the camper for vacation that we still recall with fond memories. We did a lot of weekend camping trips in between. And when Barry returned after a year, we had managed to save enough in the interim to purchase a second vehicle, this time from Peggy's other brother Frank, who had gotten it in a business deal and who gave us a really good price.

Now you can write this off as just a series of very fortuitous coincidences. You can, but I can't. I was at the time, and remain today some thirty-five years later, convinced that God engineered this whole deal to reward our faithfulness in the use of the financial resources that we were managing for Him. Now, don't get me wrong, this is not some "prosperity gospel" thing where we give in order to get. We were perfectly willing to use our (God's) savings to attend the conference and expected nothing more in return than to meet some new people and make some good contacts. Had we not been willing to make a small sacrifice, we would have likely missed out on what has become our life's calling. And we learned a valuable lesson in *Money 101* in the bargain—when you put God first in managing financial resources awesome things may happen.

Another experience several years later solidified my belief that God's ways are remarkably different from our ways, especially when it comes to finances. In 1976, Campus Crusade for Christ launched a nation-wide media project that was called the "I've Found It!" campaign. Individuals and churches in perhaps a hundred different cities in the US participated in a media outreach utilizing, bumper stickers, television and radio spots, and newspaper advertising—all featuring the slogan, "I've found it! You can find it too. New life in Jesus Christ." I agreed to head up the campaign in our city of Tuscaloosa, Alabama. We eventually mobilized forty churches of many denominations to join forces with a total budget of $40,000. $40,000! In 1976, $40,000 was a lot of money—it still is. As city director my main task was to recruit people to run the entire campaign;

and the first order of business was to recruit a finance director whose job it would be to raise the $40,000 from churches and individuals in the city.

Campus Crusade had a policy that the financial director in each city had to contribute a minimum of $5,000 toward the campaign. It didn't matter whether the city budget was $1,000,000 or $25,000, the financial director had to contribute $5,000 period. And until someone was recruited with $5,000 to invest who would also agree to raise the rest of the budget, the city director was stuck with raising the funds. I only knew two businessmen in Tuscaloosa, Alabama, who, in my judgment, had those kinds of resources. So I made an appointment with each of these men and challenged them to head up the financial part of the campaign, and to contribute $5,000 for the privilege. The reaction from both men was the same. They liked the program, but the admission fee was too high for them. So for the entire campaign I served the dual role of city director and financial director—without, of course, making the $5,000 contribution. During the three month run up to the media week, I must have spoken in 20 or 30 churches throughout the city and surrounding area. Everywhere I spoke, I outlined the program, challenged individuals and churches to involvement in the campaign, and challenged them to help underwrite the cost of the campaign.

At some point, I had to make a go/no-go decision as to whether to launch the campaign given the funding we had, the church involvement that was committed, and the manpower we had involved. Looking back, I had concerns about our ability to involve enough churches and I was concerned that we could enlist enough workers to staff the call center for the entire campaign, but I was never concerned about the money. And when the campaign started we did have the significant involvement of forty area churches and the Lord had assembled a wonderful leadership team and an army of workers for the campaign. And over the weeks leading up to the big media week, the money came in. A check in the mail one day, a pledge by telephone from a church the next day, and someone coming by the campaign center to drop off a check the following day. Gradually, dollar by dollar, the $40,000 materialized. The largest single donation we received was $2,500 from a university student who was one of my campaign leaders and who obviously believed in what we were attempting to accomplish for God! The smallest donation was a nickel from a little third grade girl who heard me speak in her church and sent her contribution in to us in an envelope, saying she wanted to give part of her allowance to help us reach her city for Christ! We were all profoundly touched when we read her note and tears come to my eyes today thirty years later thinking of her sacrifice for her Savior. She understood putting God first. And my college student friend understood it.

And the thing that $40,000 taught me is that money is of no consequence to God. He owns it all. When He wants to accomplish anything, anything at all, He will move in the hearts of His people in whatever ways are necessary to achieve His purposes. Ever since that time, I have never let financial considerations drive my life decisions. If I am convinced the Lord wants me to do something, that is enough. He will provide the resources that are necessary. The interesting thing about this is that on the deliberating side of the $40,000, or on the deliberating side of the $2,500, or on the deliberating side of the nickel, we can't see how God could possibly accomplish what we are considering. But on the committed side of the $40,000, or the $2,500, or the nickel, we get to see how God works and are blessed by our participation with Him in His plans. You can't experience the blessing until you are willing to make the commitment. Well that was another lesson in *Money 101*.

Do you see how this is just *Go Fast, Turn Left* applied to managing money? In all things financial, put God first; then consider everything else. This is so very different from what we observe in the world.

Here are some other things I learned in *Money 101* which demonstrate that God's approach to managing financial resources is very different from ours. For one thing, God doesn't want us to be preoccupied with things. Jesus said in the Sermon on the Mount, "For this reason I say to you, do not be worried about your life, as to what you will eat or what you will drink; nor for your body, as to what you will put on. Is not life more than food, and the body more than clothing (Matthew 6:25)?" And in the Parable of the Rich Fool, Jesus really drives home the point, "Yes, a person is a fool to store up earthly wealth but not have a rich relationship with God (Luke 12:16-21 NLT)." Even the Apostle Paul affirms this by announcing, "Not that I speak from want, for I have learned to be content in whatever circumstances I am (Philippians 4:11)."

Contrast this with the current situation in this country. Recently the federal government announced that in 2005 Americans spent $46 billion more than they received in wages and other income—a minus 0.5 percent savings rate. Total consumer debt in the U.S. is 1.7 trillion dollars—$8,562 per person. The average American consumer has 8 credit cards and 20 percent of these are maxed out. These statistics clearly show that we live in an age of materialism; people are madly pursuing meaning and happiness in life through the accumulation of things—from Starbucks to Hummers. Our neighbors are intent on filling the emptiness of their lives with stuff.

So two important questions for believers are (1) how do we use financial resources without being caught up in the whole materialistic scene in which those around us are so entangled and (2) for those who have not been managing financial resources Biblically, how does one manage to change habit patterns, especially if one is living beyond one's means? We discovered early on through a seminar offered at our church by Crown Financial Ministries some very solid principles that all believers ought to follow in managing financial resources. [Obviously, I am a big fan of Crown Financial Ministries and if you need some thorough assistance in this area of your life, I would highly recommend one of their small-group studies.] First of all it is necessary that we begin with a *Go Fast, Turn Left* mindset in our approach to financial resource management; then we can fill in with appropriate management and control techniques to help us succeed in this area.

How does one develop a *Go Fast, Turn Left* mindset toward financial resources? If you were to truly put God first in the financial area of your life, without regard to existing constraints or indebtedness, what would that look like? You may be presently unemployed. You may be so far in debt that the $8,562 credit card debt amount I cited previously sounds like solvency. Whatever your present situation, if you truly were able to put God first in your financial affairs, what would that entail? What level of annual (or monthly) giving would that translate into; what assets do you own that you might consider donating now or in the future to Christian ministries? Perhaps you could write out a description of this as an aspiration that you, with God's involvement, will endeavor to accomplish. The Apostle Paul gave similar advice when he wrote, "Each one must do just as he has purposed in his heart, not grudgingly or under compulsion, for God loves a cheerful giver (2 Corinthians 9:7)."

Now, while we are on the subject of giving, we might as well talk about the elephant that is in the room with us. If one truly wishes to honor God above all else in his or her finances, how much should one give to Christian ministries? A couple of definitions are in order here. The concept of the *tithe* is well-established in Scripture, beginning as early as Genesis 14:18-20 which tells us that the patriarch Abraham gave a tenth of the spoils of one of his victories to the King of Salem—an Old Testament designation for Jesus Christ. Many Christians believe that the tithe is to be the starting point for giving; in other words, we should be giving at least ten percent of our income to Christian works. An *offering* in Scripture is typically anything given over and above the tithe and indicates a desire on the part of the giver to give in extra measure perhaps for a special need or just as a token of one's love to communicate deep appreciation to a kind and generous God.

Occasionally, people ask, "Is the tithe calculated on income before taxes or is it calculated on after tax income?" To even pose the question, in my opinion, is a good sign because it shows that one is getting serious about the issue. Here is what I have concluded; I hope it is helpful. If God truly occupies first place in my financial decisions, my attitude will always be how I can give Him *more*, not *less*! Jesus certainly implied this in His answer to the Pharisees when they asked Him if it was lawful for the Jews to pay taxes to the Romans in Matthew 22:15-22 and He responded, "Give to Caesar what is Caesar's, and to God what is God's." Somehow I don't think God would be impressed if we let Caesar's part diminish God's. And the fact that Jesus did not launch into a mini-math lesson indicates, at least to me, that He fully expected us to be able to figure out what is an appropriate amount for the Lord.

Fortunately, Peggy and I had three people in our lives who thoroughly modeled generous giving. The first was a man named R.G. LeTourneau and the other two were Peggy's mother and dad, the late Frances and Wearon Huckaby of Toccoa, Georgia. We did not personally know Mr. LeTourneau, but as I shall relate, he had a large influence on us in this area. R.G. Letourneau was a multi-millionaire industrialist who made a fortune as an inventor and manufacturer of very large earth-moving machinery. In his autobiography [**R.G. LeTourneau: Mover of Men and Mountains**, Englewood Cliffs, NJ: Prentice Hall, 1960], LeTourneau describes how his first business venture, which he launched as an unbeliever, ended in bankruptcy. He became a Christian shortly before establishing the enterprise from which he would make his fortune and he determined to make God the CEO of his company. He began to tithe his income and as the business prospered in partnership as he describes it with God, he began to give a larger and larger share of the profits to the Lord's work. For many years before he died he and his wife gave 90 percent of their income to Christian work and lived on the remaining 10 percent. He liked to joke that it was a different form of tithing.

Peggy's father started working for the LeTourneau Company in Toccoa, Georgia, in the 1930s and he ultimately became a test driver for

Mr. LeTourneau, whom he affectionately called Mr. R.G. They traveled together occasionally during the War years with Mr. R.G. making calls on various government agencies and Huck (as everyone, including me, called Mr. Huckaby) demonstrating the abilities of LeTourneau's wonderful machines. Later, Huck established his own highway construction company and became a very successful businessman in his own right. But Huck and Frances had learned their lessons well under Mr. R.G.—they were without doubt the most generous people I have ever had the pleasure to know. At both of their funerals when they passed away, many people came up to us and shared how either Huck or Frances had helped them financially or otherwise without fanfare; usually without even telling the other what they had done. For many years prior to their passing the Huckabys gave over a third of their income to Christian ministries.

Given these wonderful role models, when Peggy and I started to grow as believers, we naturally decided that we needed to tithe. It was not easy when we first started, but one of the things we learned at that first Crown seminar we attended really helped. "To demonstrate that your intention is to put God first in your finances, write the checks for your tithes and offerings first before you write the other checks," we were advised. "This way, there will be no possibility of you disposing of your other bills and having nothing left over to give the Lord." So we have always done this, even today when we have a surplus and the possibility of running out is remote and we are converting many of our accounts to auto-payment options, we still write our checks for the Lord's work first. By the way, this is a Scriptural principle, Proverbs 3:9,10 encourages us to, "Honor the LORD from your wealth and from the *first* of all your produce; so your barns will be filled with plenty and your vats will overflow with new wine." [Emphasis mine]

There is a very interesting promise in the last book of the Old Testament that deals with this whole issue of putting God first in the financial area of our lives. The prophet Malachi, speaking for God, says, "Bring the whole tithe into the storehouse, so that there may be food in My house, and test Me now in this," says the LORD of hosts, "if I will not open for you the windows of heaven and pour out for you a blessing until it overflows (Malachi 3:10)." And Jesus Himself echoed the same promise in His teaching, "Give, and it will be given to you. A good measure, pressed down, shaken together and running over, will be poured into your lap. For with the measure you use, it will be measured to you (Luke 6:38 NIV)." Now, as I have already mentioned, we don't give in order to get; we give because we love God and we want to do all that we can in order to further

His work. For His part, God has promised to abundantly bless those who put Him first in this area. Peggy and I have been well beyond tithing for many years and we can both attest to the faithfulness of God in this regard—and the greatest blessing of our commitment has not necessarily been financial, although we have experienced that, but just the pure joy of participating with God in reaching a lost world for Christ.

Once we have begun to grasp the notion of putting God first in our financial affairs and have articulated what we are purposing to accomplish in this area and are beginning to take some positive steps in this direction, then it is time to begin to consider some practical management and control techniques to help us succeed in our aspirations. This is especially important for those who may have been struggling with finances. Interestingly, most financial advisors, even secular ones, suggest that for individuals who are struggling in the financial area, the answer is generally not to earn more [this is usually not a viable option for most people] but to do a better job of managing the money they do earn.

Of course, one of the first things many financial advisors teach is the value of developing a budget and—this is important—following it. Developing a budget is the easy part [good resources are readily available to help you accomplish this] the difficult part is learning to live by the budget. Here is a funny story of how we were able to take some of the things we learned in our first financial management seminar and implement them effectively in our life. The seminar leader showed us how to apply appropriate percentages to our monthly income to ascertain how much we could afford to spend in various categories—giving, saving, insurance, housing, medical, groceries, etc. Then he showed us one of the simplest and most effective control techniques: at the first of each month, we were advised to cash a check for the entire month's groceries and miscellaneous allocation. The funds were then to be divided and placed into eight envelopes marked, "Groceries—Week 1," "Miscellaneous—Week 1," "Groceries—Week 2," and so on. As we had expenditures for groceries or miscellaneous items through the month, we would simply remove money from the appropriate envelope. The great beauty of this system is that when there is no longer any money in one of the envelopes, it is perfectly clear what action to take. You simply don't spend any more that week on that category. An absolutely foolproof system. Here's how well the system worked. Years after we took the course, I used to tell my students at the university, "If you are ever in the checkout line at the grocery store behind a middle-age lady who is rifling through several white envelopes for her money, just say, 'Hello, Mrs. Mellichamp,' because that's my wife."

If you have never learned the discipline of planning a budget and following it as you make financial decisions, I would encourage you to do so. This is another bit of wisdom I have picked up over the years in *Money 101*.

Before we wrap this up, I want to recommend a really great book in the personal financial management area. This particular book is not a Christian book, so it necessarily omits what is the most important aspect of financial management—that of putting God first in our finances. Apart from this omission [which is not a problem for us because we now understand this important consideration], it contains some of the best advice about wealth accumulation I have ever read. The book is *The Millionaire Next Door* [Thomas J. Stanley and William D. Danko, *The Millionaire Next Door*, NY, NY: Pocket Books, 1996]. Stanley and Danko disclose in this very well researched book how the wealthiest individuals in America have become wealthy. We recognize that our ultimate goal in the financial area is not to accumulate wealth, but to be good stewards of the resources God has entrusted to us. We want to hear the commendation of Jesus when we stand before Him, "Well done, good and faithful servant (Matthew 25:14-21)." After reading the book, I bought a copy for each of our grown children and told them, "Read this and do what they say."

I will close this chapter by commenting on another passage from Matthew's Gospel. Jesus told His followers in the Sermon on the Mount, "Do not store up for yourselves treasures on earth, where moth and rust destroy, and where thieves break in and steal. But store up for yourselves treasures in heaven, where neither moth nor rust destroys, and where thieves do not break in or steal; for where your treasure is, there your heart will be also (Matthew 6:19-21)." This is simply another way of telling us to have a *Go Fast, Turn Left* attitude toward financial resources. When you begin to think about finances in this way, perhaps R.G. LeTourneau's approach to tithing was not so radical after all.

Questions

1.   Have you ever thought at all about putting God first in all of your financial decisions? Do you personally know anyone who has done this or who you think might be doing it?

2. Can you think of anything that would hinder your adopting a *Go Fast, Turn Left* attitude toward finances? What would be necessary to remove these constraints to following God's design for you in this area? Are you willing to trust God to enable you to remove them?

3. What would it look like if you truly began to put God first, above everything else, in the financial area of your life? Would you be willing today, right now, to begin to start making some tangible steps in that direction?

4. Have you ever thought about where you would like to be in the financial area of your life five, ten, or twenty years down the road? Where does God fit into these financial dreams of yours? Did He even enter the picture before reading this chapter?

5. Based on some of the concepts we have discussed in this chapter, what legacy would you like to leave in the financial area? What do you think it would be important to have accomplished in this area in your lifetime?

GO FAST, TURN LEFT
Availability

One of my favorite books is *The Call: Finding and Fulfilling the Central Purpose of Your Life* by Os Guinness [Os Guinness, *The Call: Finding and Fulfilling the Central Purpose of Your Life,* Nashville, TN: Word Publishing, 1998]. Normally when I read a book, I highlight what to me are important points or sentences with a yellow highlighter. When I finished reading this book for the first time, I had highlighted practically every word in the book! Even so, one particular thought impressed me profoundly, because it so aptly describes my fourth life lesson— availability. Guinness writes, "The truth is not that God is finding us a place for our gifts but that God has created us and our gifts for a place of His choosing—and we will only be ourselves when we are there." This is a remarkable insight! God is not looking around for a place to use us and our gifts as many believers probably imagine He does as He assigns us to our various places. He created me and gave me different natural abilities and spiritual gifts specifically for a place He had in mind for me from eternity past! And He created and gifted you for just such a unique place as well. When we put ourselves at God's disposal, when we make ourselves *available* to Him to use however He sees fit, then and only then will we be what we were created to be.

I first started getting a glimpse of this as a young professor in the university, and I still remember the event which precipitated this insight as though it were yesterday. I was walking across campus one afternoon soon after joining the faculty at the University of Alabama. As I walked, I recalled having read the obituary of a prominent professor in the local newspaper the previous evening. This man—whose name I have long forgotten—was well-known enough that his obituary started on the front page of the paper and continued on the obituary page. In all, the notice was probably 10 or 12 column inches. Listed were all of his academic accomplishments: his degrees and the universities from which they were obtained; all of the positions he had held in academe; many scholarly publications; various committee assignments and task force memberships; and much more. There were a few mentions of family: his wife and children, a relative or two. I looked carefully, but saw no mention whatever of anything religious; no mention of a church affiliation, no religious involvement at all, nothing.

31

As I walked and reflected, it occurred to me that none of the "stuff" he had done was of much benefit to him then. Now don't misunderstand what I'm saying. For a professor, these things are terribly important. But these worldly trappings are not the bottom line. They are not and should not be the sum and substance of our lives, which appeared to be the case for the gentleman whose obituary I was considering. As I continued to walk and think, I wondered what I would like for my obituary to say about me at the end of my life. I decided I would want it to say a lot about how I had used my influence as a professor for Christ, to cause students and colleagues to consider Him, and to influence the university for good and noble causes. And I came to the conclusion that if I was not faithful to represent Christ through my university position, if I was not available for Him to use in my different spheres of influence, God could jolly well raise up someone else with all the necessary qualifications, gifts, and abilities who would faithfully represent Him in my place. That is to say, I started seeing that God had put me in that place to be His representative. He could have created anyone for the position, but He created me. How could I not try to faithfully represent Him there?

Now you may be wondering what this all has to do with you. It has everything to do with you. Most likely you are not a university professor. It doesn't matter. Let me paraphrase the last part of Guinness' quote, "God has created you and your gifts for a place of His choosing—and you will only be yourself when you are there." Regardless of your situation, God has a special, unique place for you. Perhaps you are a stay-at-home mom; God has a special place for you. It might be reaching out to other moms through a kids play group. Perhaps you are a factory worker. God has a special place for you. How are you representing Jesus to other workers in the workplace? Perhaps you are a student. God has a special place for you. Have you identified other Christian students in your school and are you working together with them to have an influence for Christ there? Perhaps you are a professional. God has a special place for you. What are you doing and being to represent Jesus in your profession?

Some years ago, someone in our ministry had the bright idea that we could get more professors involved in our efforts if we had them excluded from church involvement with the excuse that many church members could work in the church, but only a few had access to and influence on the university campus. So those who had access to the campus should work exclusively on the campus and those who didn't should sing in the choir, teach Sunday school, serve on committees, etc. When I first heard this, I was incredulous! This is tantamount to saying, "God only

32

expects professors to have a ministry outside of the church; everyone else is excused!" As I understand the Great Commission, as expressed in Matthew 28:18-20 and Acts 1:8, Jesus expects all of His followers to go and make disciples, not just some isolated ones here or there and He expects all to be faithful workers in His church as well. So I was able to get this faulty logic set aside in favor of a truly Biblical view. The clear message from Scripture is that God has a special place for you in the world where He intends to use you to reach the lost and to exercise a presence for good—to be salt and light.

So the important thing, the *Go Fast, Turn Left* thing, is to discover the place God has for us and make ourselves *available* to Him, trusting Him to use us in a transforming way in that place. And the really important question for us is how do we discover the place God has created us for so that we can begin to be and do what He wants of us in that place? Hugh Ross, a friend of mine, started a ministry twenty years ago and in a recent ministry letter he gives a simple piece of advice for discovering the place God has for us [*Reasons to Believe*, February 2006 letter]. "When God says, 'Follow Me,' it's best to get moving even if you can't imagine how you're going to do what He's called you to do." Hugh's point is that when we sense that God may be calling us into a particular activity or area, to simply begin to move forward, whatever that might mean. If God is truly calling you to that place, He will make it known to you. What you are doing will be consistent with Scripture, others will affirm you, and you yourself will begin to experience a satisfaction in your involvement. Let me give you a couple of personal examples to illustrate.

When I returned home from our first Christian faculty conference at Arrowhead Springs, California, in 1970, I knew that if professors were going to have any influence for Jesus on the campus, it would be important to begin to get all of the Christian faculty members at the university together. I didn't really have any definite ideas about what we could or would do, but my background as an industrial engineer convinced me that we needed to work together synergistically as Christ's representatives on campus. So I went to the two men whom I thought would be ideal candidates to lead such a group. Both were full professors [their jobs were safe and I viewed this as a dangerous undertaking], both were well-known in the community and on campus as Christians, and both were well-respected in the university. When I shared with each man individually my idea of getting the Christian faculty on campus together, they both had the same reaction, "Why would we want to do that?" Since I hadn't thought through my strategy entirely—and indeed the purpose of meeting together was exactly to formulate a strategy—I had to tell them I didn't know. Given my uncertainty, I can't blame them for turning me down as they both did.

So I switched to Plan B, which really wasn't a plan at all. I began meeting weekly for lunch with two young assistant professors my own age, one from the school of education and the other from the music department. We prayed for the university and its leaders, and we talked about how we could represent Jesus in our teaching and research and in our everyday lives on campus. And gradually, over several years, we grew until we had a list of the names of 75-80 Christian faculty and staff members at the university and 15-20 of us were meeting weekly. In the process, we worked out the basics of what we now call a Christian Faculty Forum or Fellowship. There are currently 200-300 such groups on university and college campuses in this country and abroad. And these groups have influenced thousands of college students and professors for Christ and have had a substantial influence in restoring truth to universities and colleges and confronting some of the wrong-headed ideas that arise on university campuses these days. One of the long-range goals of our ministry is to establish similar groups at every one of the top 151 [research] universities in the United States—we are currently at about half of them. Interestingly, both of the men I approached about leading the group subsequently became members of our group. One of them even commented a few years later when we were writing the editor of the local newspaper to offer a counter view to some relevant issue, "You know, I can see how a group like this could really have an influence for good in the university and in the culture!"

Here is the important point in this illustration. I never aspired to be a leader of Christian professors on my campus nor in the United States nor in the world. But I wanted to be faithful to whatever God had called me to be and do in my university. When He started impressing on me the importance of meeting together with my Christian faculty colleagues to think about how we could represent Him in academia, I started moving. Without a plan. Without a strategy. Taking small steps at first. Doing dumb things. Remembering not to do the same dumb things again. Until over the years, I discovered the place for which God created and gifted me. It has been exciting. It has been frustrating. It has been challenging. It is still daunting. But it has brought a tremendous sense of purpose and fulfillment to my life—it is truly my call. Have you found your call? If you have, wonderful; if not start moving as you sense God leading and make yourself available to Him. He will direct you there.

Here is another story which illustrates that when you make yourself available and start moving in response to God's call, you are in for an exciting ride. In March 1986, Christian Leadership Ministries sponsored *Artificial Intelligence and the Human Mind*, an international, interdisciplinary conference at Yale University to explore the question, "Is the human mind more than a complex computer?" Many of the top researchers in artificial intelligence, medicine, psychology, and related fields, including three Nobel Laureates and three of the most important figures in launching the artificial intelligence effort in this country, were invited to present papers. At the time, I had been doing research in the field for two or three years in an applied area. So when I learned of the Yale conference in October or November of 1985, I mentioned to the director of our ministry, that I would really like to attend. He said that he would talk to the conference organizer and get an official invitation for me. So, I made a mental note that I would be going to the conference in March and promptly forgot about it.

I recall returning home from a family Christmas trip and going through the mountain of mail that had accumulated while we were away. There was a lot of junk mail that I stacked in a pile to go through later. Several days later, sometime around New Year's, I began opening and disposing of the last stack. Imagine my surprise when one of the letters contained not only an invitation to the Yale conference, but also a conference bulletin listing my name as one of the twenty invited speakers! My initial reaction was that someone had made a mistake. A big mistake! Then it slowly dawned on me that this was no mistake and my reaction immediately turned to horror. I was going to get killed. I had never done any research in the area of human intelligence. My research was limited to attempting to apply some of the methodology of artificial intelligence in manufacturing and communications. I had never even thought about the human mind in relation to fast, complex computers. Of course, it immediately occurred to me that my answer, as a Christian, to the conference question was that there is indeed a vast difference between human intelligence and machine intelligence.

The more I thought about my predicament, the more I realized that this was an incredible opportunity for the cause of Christ. I was convinced that most, if not all, of the presenters would come down on the side of materialism and argue that the human mind is nothing more than a very fast, very sophisticated computer—"a meat machine" as one researcher in the field had often described it. The thought also crossed my mind that if I turned down this opportunity to make a bold stand for Christ in the scientific community before some of the really big names in the field, I would have no one to blame but myself if I never had another chance. Peggy affirmed this idea in exactly the same terms. But, it was less than ten weeks until the conference. How could I possibly read everything necessary to present a strong argument? How could I ever expect to gain any ground for the Christian worldview against such odds? If I failed, I was risking professional embarrassment.

Regardless, I determined to accept the challenge. For the next ten weeks, I did little else but read, read, read. And I puzzled over the problem. I taught my classes and saw my family at meals and for the rest of my waking hours, I holed up and devoted myself to understanding how the human mind differs from a computer. In my paper, "The *Artificial* in Artificial Intelligence is Real," I used a series of quotes from top researchers in the field to show that they themselves believe that there is a qualitative difference between human intelligence and machine intelligence, whether or not they were willing affirm this at the conference. In other words, I turned their own words against them. I must have done a creditable job, because when I went in to dinner at the conclusion of the conference right after giving my talk, Sir John Eccles, Nobel Laureate in Medicine and Physiology (1963) and easily the most respected individual present, invited me to sit next to him. As I sat down, Sir John quipped, "Professor Mellichamp, I really liked your paper. You are not crazy like all the other artificial intelligence guys are!" And then he proceeded to question me further about my views on the topic!

This was certainly the biggest risk I took in my career as a university professor. As a result, a couple of hundred key people in the scientific community, including Professor Anthony Flew, a very well-known atheist at the time, heard a Biblical position (without Biblical references) advanced in a scientific setting. I have used the ideas I argued in the paper as well as the story behind the paper dozens of times since then in academic settings in this country and abroad. None of this would have been possible, had I not made myself—with all of my inadequacies—available to be used (and possibly skewered) for the glory of God. Here is one last illustration that clearly shows how God can use us even when we are not even aware of His doing so if we are just available.

In the early 1990s, Peggy and I met a young missionary couple who were seeking to start a mission work in a closed country [not open to Christian ministries]. When they learned that our ministry frequently involved university professors on international trips to open ministry doors, they promptly invited us to bring a team to their country. Frankly, we hadn't thought at all about visiting that country, and it really wasn't very high on our list of travel destinations, but they were so sincerely interested in having us come and so optimistic about what such a trip might do for their ministry, we agreed to bring a team. We asked our Christian Leadership Ministries contacts to see whether any other professors or staff would be willing to accompany us. Apparently, they all felt the same way we did because there were no takers.

So the following summer, Peggy and I set out to spend a week with the couple in their country. The husband had set me up with two professional talks in two different universities in the country, and we had one meeting with several government officials. That was it, not very much in comparison with some of the trips we have made where we are speaking several times a day. We had a wonderful time in the country. It was beautiful; quite different from our American idea of what we would find. The presentations went well, and so did the lunch meeting. But there was no spiritual content whatsoever in anything I said or did. There could not have been for fear of jeopardizing our friends. I remember remarking to Peggy on the way home that we had wasted a lot of our time and money and didn't really have too much to show for our efforts—this was my assessment from a human perspective. Then we heard back from our missionary friends.

The husband wrote me later that he had been able to use the contacts he had made at my presentations and the meeting with the officials to develop a ministry focus that has connected him at the very highest levels of the leadership of the country. When we read the letter, the details of which I can't disclose, we saw the sovereign hand of God working through our feeble efforts to accomplish His desired ends in that land. It was absolutely miraculous. Never in our wildest imaginations could we have pictured what God was able to accomplish from our visit. And it is a good thing. I would have been so proud of myself! As it turned out, all we could do was shake our heads and say, "God did it all and to Him be the glory!" Our responsibility in all of this is to be available; God is entirely responsible for the results.

So life lesson number four is to be available to be used by God in whatever way He desires. When we live in this way, we will arrive at the place He ordained in eternity past especially for us and our lives will be filled with meaning and purpose. Every day will be an adventure as we discover His will for our lives. As the prophet Jeremiah wrote on God's behalf to the Jewish people in exile in Babylon, "'For I know the plans that I have for you,' declares the LORD, 'plans for welfare and not for calamity to give you a future and a hope (Jeremiah 29:11).'"

Questions

1. Have you ever thought about why God created you exactly as He did? About why you have the natural abilities you have? Have you discovered your spiritual gifts? If so, have you ever wondered why He gave you the spiritual gift(s) you have?

2. Can you think of anything that would hinder your adopting a *Go Fast, Turn Left* attitude toward your availability to God to be used for His purposes? What would be necessary to remove these constraints to following God's design for you in this area? Are you willing to trust God to enable you to remove them?

3. What would it look like if you truly began to move out in some area or areas in which you sense God might be leading? What would be your first steps? Would you be willing today, right now, to begin to start making some tangible steps in that direction?

4. Have you ever thought about what you would ultimately like to have said about your life? Of course, we all want to hear Jesus say, "Well done." But what specifically would you like for people to remember about your life? How would you like for people to characterize your life once you are gone?

5. Have you arrived at God's place for you? Is your life characterized by a sense of purpose and fulfillment? Are you truly available to God?

GO FAST, TURN LEFT
Discipleship

My fifth life lesson has been wonderfully verbalized by Dallas Willard in his book, *The Divine Conspiracy* [Dallas Willard, *The Divine Conspiracy: Rediscovering Our Hidden Life in God*, San Francisco, CA: HarperCollins Inc., 1998]. In answering the question, what would motivate a person to choose to become a disciple of Jesus, Willard writes, "Obviously, one would feel great admiration and love, would really believe that Jesus is the most magnificent person who has ever lived. One would be quite sure that to belong to Him, to be taken into what He is doing throughout this world so that what He is doing becomes your life, is the greatest opportunity one will ever have." Do you believe this? Willard is writing here on the topic, "On Being a Disciple, or Student, of Jesus [Chapter 8]." And he says since Jesus is the most magnificent person who ever lived, the greatest opportunity you will ever have is to become His disciple. The opportunity to be a disciple of Jesus is a greater opportunity than to study in one of the world's great universities, or to apprentice under one of the world's most powerful executives or judges, or to set a world's record in any sport, or to live and move among the political or artistic leaders of the world. In fact, think of any opportunity you will ever have in your life. Being a disciple of Jesus makes any other opportunity you have pale in comparison.

To illustrate this Willard uses two of the parables of Jesus—the Parable of the Hidden Treasure (Matthew 13:44) and the Parable of the Pearl of Great Price (Matthew 13:45-46). Willard suggests that becoming a disciple of Jesus is like a man who discovers a hidden treasure in a field; he quickly covers it up again. Overflowing with excitement he pulls together everything he has, sells it all, and buys the field. Or it is like a businessman who is on the lookout for beautiful pearls. He finds one pearl of incredible value. So he sells everything else he owns and buys it. Neither the one who found the treasure in the field nor the businessman who found the pearl was thinking about the cost of the field or the pearl. "The only thing those people were sweating about was whether they would 'get the deal,'" says Willard. If we really believed that the greatest opportunity we will ever have is to be a disciple of Jesus, we would make any sacrifice in order to do so. We would scarcely even consider what little we would have to give up in order to be with Him, to learn His ways, and to participate in His work.

Our first experience with becoming a disciple of Jesus occurred shortly after our arrival on the campus of the University of Alabama. We had been encouraged by Peggy's brother Barry to get in touch with the Campus Crusade for Christ staff on campus. Peggy did some calling around, and we finally located Rick and Laurel Langston, the campus directors of the student ministry. In January 1970, we met them for coffee. They told us later they had been praying for professors to be involved in the ministry. At the time, Peggy and I both were at point "zero" on the spiritual maturity scale. Were we ever baby Christians! Neither of us had grown at all beyond simple commitment of our lives to Christ years earlier. Rick must have recognized this because he challenged us to go through the standard training courses that all the Campus Crusade for Christ students undertake. Then, it was called Leadership Training Course (LTC)—Basic, Intermediate, and Advanced. Well, I imagined myself as a leader, so we consented to do the training. What conceit!

We attended one night a week for a year and a half with all the students—freshmen, sophomores, and a few juniors and seniors. Our children were in grammar school then, and they went with us. They would sit in the back of the class and do their homework and then read comic books, color, or whatever. And they loved it. The college students made a big deal over them and, of course, the children thought the college students were the greatest. All the while, Peggy and I were learning about assurance of salvation, the ministry of the Holy Spirit in the life of the believer, how to share our faith with an unbeliever, how to have a quiet time, how to write our personal testimony—all of the things a disciple of Jesus needs to know. By the end of that year and a half, we were pretty well along on the path to spiritual maturity.

It was the equipping we received in those early years that has enabled Peggy and me to give leadership to numerous Christian endeavors since then. Earlier, in the chapter on money, I mentioned the "I've Found It" campaign that I directed in our city. Had we not previously been well-grounded in the basics of the faith I would not have felt capable of directing the effort. Interestingly, in the process of doing the campaign, I gravitated into a style of leadership that I can only describe as discipleship-oriented. Here is how that happened. Following the manuals we were given by Campus Crusade to execute the campaign, I divided the city and surrounding area into six or seven geographical areas and recruited a friend or acquaintance to give direction to each of the areas. We were all young businessmen or professionals in the 30-40 age range. Within a few weeks of beginning our efforts, six or eight of us started meeting together early one morning each week to report on activities and to pray for the campaign. Then, it seemed the natural thing to grab breakfast together before heading into work. So we started doing breakfast together at a local café.

Pretty soon someone asked if I would do a short devotional to start our meeting times together—I thought that was a good idea and I had heard that the book of Nehemiah contained some good principles of leadership, so I started sharing with the guys from Nehemiah's account of rebuilding the wall around Jerusalem after the Babylonian captivity. One day, someone in the group observed that our mission in conducting the city-wide campaign was the spiritual equivalent of Nehemiah's task of rebuilding the Jerusalem wall—so we became the *Wallbuilders*. Weeks before the media campaign started, the *Wallbuilders* were on our knees at least one morning each week praying earnestly that the Lord would give us success in building a hedge around our city.

I can't tell you how those sessions impacted each member of the group—we were accountable to each other; for our assignments, for our spiritual lives, for our families, for our testimonies in the community. And the bond that formed among us was awesome. We started having a regular social time with our wives and children—picnics and cookouts. And we became best of friends. Thirty years later, I still credit Dennis Painter, Richard Thomason, Harold Guy, Ron Duff, Nelson Ford, Charlie Van Eaton, Jim Allen Randall, Mike Parker and Randy Leavitt with having had a significant impact on my spiritual development, because we were all willing to be honest with one another and to challenge one another to be committed followers of Jesus. We continued meeting together for several years—long after the media campaign was successfully completed. I am still in touch with several of these men after all these years and consider them to be true brothers in the Lord.

Unfortunately, many believers have not had the wonderful opportunities to be discipled that Peggy and I had. I have been involved in adult education in churches for the past 35 years and I meet very few Christians who have been thoroughly grounded in the basic doctrines and practices of the Christian faith. To me, perhaps the greatest failing of the Christian community in the modern era is that it has lost its focus on discipleship. Discipleship was the means Jesus employed to install his Kingdom; His last instructions to his own disciples in what we call the Great Commission were, "Go therefore and make disciples of all the nations, baptizing them in the name of the Father and the Son and the Holy Spirit, teaching them to observe all that I commanded you; and lo, I am with you always, even to the end of the age (Matthew 28:19-20)." As Robert Coleman puts it in *The Master Plan of Evangelism* [Robert E. Coleman, *The Master Plan of Evangelism*, Old Tappan, NJ: Fleming H. Revell Company, 1963], "His concern was not programs to reach the multitudes, but men whom the multitudes would follow." And A.B. Bruce enlarges on this approach in *The Training of the Twelve* [Alexander Balmain Bruce, *The Training of the Twelve*, Grand Rapids, MI: Kregel Publications, 1988], "Eventually they would be Christ's chosen agents, fully trained to spread the faith after He left the earth. ... In this course of training, they were to learn what they should do, believe, and teach as His witnesses and ambassadors to the world."

The Apostle Paul certainly understood the mandate to make disciples both from an individual perspective and from the perspective of the church. He wrote what might be called his own life purpose statement, "We proclaim Him, admonishing every man and teaching every man with all wisdom, so that we may present every man complete [mature] in Christ (Colossians 1:28)." And he described the process to his own young disciple, Timothy, "The things which you have heard from me in the presence of many witnesses, entrust these to faithful men who will be able to teach others also (2 Timothy 2:2)." Paul's view of the role of the church was as follows: "And He gave some as apostles, and some as prophets, and some as evangelists, and some as pastors and teachers, for the equipping of the saints for the work of service, to the building up of the body of Christ; until we all attain to the unity of the faith, and of the knowledge of the Son of God, to a mature man, to the measure of the stature which belongs to the fullness of Christ (Ephesians 4:11-13)." Somehow we have lost this focus on discipling believers and in the process, in my opinion, we have become populated with believers who don't know what they believe—with soldiers who are not equipped to engage in spiritual warfare.

So my advice to you in this respect is simple: make sure that you are truly a disciple of Jesus. Remember these two *Go Fast, Turn Left* principles:

1. The greatest opportunity you will ever have is to become a disciple of Jesus.
2. Every other opportunity you will ever have is a distant second to discipleship.

The real question then becomes, "How does one go about becoming a disciple of Jesus?" Discipleship takes place in life-on-life encounters in one-on-one or one-on-few (small group) environments. You will never become an equipped follower of Jesus by sitting in a large congregation (or a small one for that matter) on Sunday mornings listening to sermons. Discipleship requires effort and accountability; neither of these happens unless it is intentionally embedded in some kind of structured environment.

So as you consider how to become a true disciple of Jesus, look for opportunities to participate in one-on-one or small-group environments in which you can be accountable to another believer or other believers for your life, including your spiritual growth. If there are no such programs available in your church, perhaps you could go to your pastor and ask him if he would consider starting one. The church we attend is a huge mega-church in Atlanta with over 4,000 members; the motto of the church is "Making mature and equipped followers of Christ for the lost world." Over 1,500 of our members are involved in life-on-life discipleship groups using a three-year curriculum that the church developed. Our pastor Randy Pope, whom I first knew as a fellow member of a Campus Crusade discipleship group when he was a student at the University of Alabama, shares his view on the importance of discipleship in the local church in his book *The Prevailing Church* [Randy Pope, *The Prevailing Church*, Chicago, IL: Moody Press, 2002], the church's "primary outreach, nurture, education, care, discipline, and equipping take place in small groups where the leader is considered the pastor and the community out of which the participants come (residential, relational, professional, or social) is considered the mission field." Randy would be the first person to tell you that the success of our church is because of its commitment to discipleship. Several years ago, in celebrating the twenty-fifth anniversary of the church, we made an intentional decision to "give the church away"—part of that involves resourcing other churches. So if you or your pastor or others in your church would like more information on how a church can truly embrace discipleship, check out our church Web Site at www.perimeter.org.

In January of 2003, I asked Randy to do the devotional at a regional conference of Christian professors our ministry was hosting in Atlanta. He asked what I wanted him to focus on in his comments. Since one of our biggest challenges in working with busy professionals is getting them to see the campus as their part of the mission field, I replied that anything he could suggest to build their commitment to ministering through their teaching and research would be appropriate. Randy showed up at an airport hotel a few weeks later for the conference and gave a simple talk on discipleship that I had heard him give often at the church. Frankly, I was mildly disappointed that we had missed a good opportunity to ratchet up the commitment level of some of our best professors. Then, the following month on the way home from an international ministry trip, I decided to spend part of the flight reflecting on our ministry and trying to pinpoint why our professors were not more committed to reaching their universities for Christ. Guess what I came up with? They haven't been discipled. Randy had been right on target with his talk.

This led to the development of a two-year small group discipleship curriculum for Christian professors aimed at equipping them as believers to represent Jesus on their campuses through their teaching and research. It includes such things as how to have a devotional time, how to share their faith with unbelievers, how to write their testimony, how to effectively manage their time, some basic apologetics, and a host of other things that they don't learn in graduate school and they haven't learned in their churches. We are now utilizing this material throughout our ministry and have a strategic goal to "equip 2,500 Christian professors as mature faculty leaders through small-group discipleship programs" over the next five years. Beginning in August of 2004 I led a group of four senior professors and one senior research engineer at Georgia Tech through the curriculum and Peggy led a group of two women professors from Tech and two wives of Tech professors through the process. What a thrill to see them growing in their faith and commitment level as they were exposed to basic Christian instruction and when several of them started their own discipleship groups of other Tech professors we saw 2 Timothy 2:2 being fulfilled before our very eyes!

If Christianity is to remain an influencing force in Western culture, I believe, it will be because the body of Christ rediscovers an emphasis on discipleship. It will happen, as Coleman puts it, as we disciple men and women "whom the multitudes will follow." So, if you haven't already attended to this, my parting advice to you is "get yourself discipled!"

Questions

1. Have you ever been discipled by another Christian? If you have been discipled, what sorts of topics were included in the training? What was the nature of accountability used to ensure that assignments were completed and material mastered?

2. If you have never been personally discipled by another believer, can you think of anything you could do that could have a greater impact on

your spiritual growth and maturity? Are there any reasons why you should not seek to be discipled now?

3. If you have never been discipled, what would it require in terms of commitment on your part to be discipled? What kind of time and energy commitment would it require? If you really believe this is the greatest opportunity you will ever have, wouldn't it be worth any sacrifice in terms of time and energy?

4. If you have never been discipled and are now open to the possibility of doing so, are there opportunities for discipleship at your local church? If so, is there any reason you couldn't begin the next time sessions are started? If there are no options available, would your pastor be open to initiating something? Perhaps you could check the perimeter.org Web Site to get him some information prior to asking.

5. Have you ever discipled someone else? Can you think of anything you could do for another person that could have a greater impact on his or her spiritual growth and maturity than to become a spiritual mentor for them?

6. If you have never discipled another person, would you be open to the possibility of doing so? Are there opportunities for participating in such activities at your church? If not, would you be willing to initiate something?

7. What about your workplace, or neighborhood, or social circle, or family connections? Could you see yourself leading a discipleship group in one of those contexts?

GO FAST, TURN LEFT
Epilog

Well, there you have it—*Go Fast, Turn Left*—the five most important lessons God has taught me in many years of walking with Him:

1. Jesus is to be the *priority* of my life.
2. I need to make the most of my *time*.
3. I am to be a steward of the Lord's *money*.
4. God has a unique place for me if I'm *available*.
5. I need to be *discipled* to be effective.

Understanding these five things has made a huge difference in my life. Not that I have mastered all five of them, I am still working on them and I won't have them all down pat until my life here is over. But just knowing them and working on them has enabled me to move ahead with confidence that one day I will hear the commendation, "Well done."

I hope these lessons will be useful to you as you follow Jesus. I have had to write using the university as a backdrop because I have lived most of my life in the university. But as I said earlier, it makes no difference what your life situation is, these lessons apply to all who would live purposefully for Jesus. If you are a self-employed businessman or woman, you need to make Jesus the priority of your life. Whether you are a professional or work in a factory, you need to make the most of your time, especially the time you have away from the job. If you are married or single, you need to see yourself as a steward of the Lord's resources. Whatever your life situation or circumstances, God created and gifted you for a place of His choosing and you will not be truly fulfilled until you discover what and where that is. And all believers, even kids, need to become devoted disciples of the One they follow.

So I hope that you haven't thought as you have read these lessons, "Oh, I don't work in an academic setting, or I don't have a university degree so none of this applies to me." I hope that as you have read and considered, you have come to the conclusion that these five things are all very important to anyone who is serious about following Jesus. One good thing about me being a professor though is that professors are paid to think about stuff and I have spent a lot of time thinking about the things God has been teaching me. And I now have the opportunity to share some of my experiences with you. If this has been too academic or too much about the university, I apologize and ask you to look beyond the illustrations and the experiences and discover the principles I have tried to point out and the applications that might be helpful to your own life. If you will do this, these things may become your life lessons also. I hope they will.

I have another reason for wanting to share these lessons with you. For most of my Christian life I have been concerned with the idea of models. We need models of how to live Christianly—people who are like us, perhaps a bit older, who have traveled the same road and successfully negotiated the challenges of life. As I wrote in *Ministering in the Secular University*, [Joseph McRae Mellichamp, *Ministering in the Secular University: A Guide for Christian Professors and Staff*, Carrollton, TX: Lewis and Stanley, 1997]:

> Looking back over my career, I think the most difficult aspect of it was there were no role models for me to follow. ... For me, there were no models of what it was to be a Christian professor. What is a Christian professor? What does one look like? What does one do? What differentiates a Christian professor from any other professor or from a professor who just happens to be a Christian? Many times in my career, I would have welcomed the chance to just look over at Dr. Christian, Professor of Engineering or Professor of History, who was a model of what I needed to become: someone who was succeeding in his teaching and research and who was having an impact for Christ on the institution and on his students and colleagues; someone who had it together in his family and in his church; someone who was respected as a Christian man or woman in the university, in the church, and in the community. There was no one. ... So one of the things I wanted to accomplish in my career was to be an example of what a Christian professor is to younger professors and staff, and older ones, too, if they were interested.

And one of the things I wanted to accomplish by writing down my life lessons was to encourage others who are coming along behind me. To share some of the wisdom I have picked up along the way and, perhaps, to be a role model for them. By the way, this is a Biblical concept. The Apostle Paul wrote, "Now these things happened to them as an example, and they were written for our instruction, upon whom the ends of the ages have come (1 Corinthians 10:11)." The Scriptures are replete with examples of men and women; some of whom lived victoriously for Jesus and some of whom crashed and burned on the journey. God included them in His word to be examples for us. I believe we also need modern day examples and illustrations of how to live wholeheartedly for Jesus. So I am offering these experiences, for what they are worth, from someone who has been down the road and perhaps learned some valuable lessons.

One last thing and I am done. Perhaps as you have read these lessons, you have realized that you really don't have a personal relationship with Jesus—you don't know Him the way I have been describing. That's OK. I intended to write for a Christian audience and I have presumed that my readers were just that. Perhaps as you have read, you've thought, "I'd really like to live like that. I'd like to live a life of meaning and purpose. I'd like to discover the unique place for which God created and gifted me. I'd like to become a true disciple of Jesus—that might be the greatest opportunity I'll ever have." Well you can do all of these things. It all starts by recognizing that you are separated from God, by either active rebellion or passive indifference, and by affirming that you want to have a relationship with Him. God has already done everything necessary through the death and resurrection of His Son for you to have an eternal relationship with Him. You see, Jesus died to pay the penalty for your rejection of God—for all of the things that you have said and done and thought that separated you from Him. All you have to do is to accept God's offer of love and forgiveness through Jesus. And you can do that right now, right where you are. If you truly desire to know God in a personal way, you can commit your life to Him as your Savior and Lord and begin an eternal relationship with Him. Here is a prayer you might pray to God to accept His offer of love and forgiveness:

Father, I recognize that I have been alienated from you by my attitudes, words, and actions. I am sorry. Please forgive me as You promise in Your word You will. I ask You now to be my Lord and Savior, take up residence in my life now and begin to change me into the person You want me to be. Thank You. Amen.

If you truly desired to know God in a personal way and you prayed that little prayer, God will honor that and begin to work in your life. You might want to share what you have done with a Christian friend or with your pastor and ask if he or she will help you to begin to grow in your new relationship with God. Oh, and one more thing. Don't forget as you begin your new life in Jesus to *Go Fast, Turn Left*.

49

Note: Additional copies of *Go Fast, Turn Left* can be purchased online at: http://clmstore.stores.yahoo.net

APPENDIX 1
The Quiet Time

For the Christian, two questions are of primary importance. They are the same questions asked of the Lord by the Apostle Paul on the road to Damascus (Acts 22:8.10). "Who are You, Lord?" and "What shall I do, Lord?" The believer who is seeking answers to these questions on a daily basis will be experiencing a dynamic personal relationship with Christ, moving toward maturity as a disciple.

How does one discover answers to these questions? The Apostle John gives us the answer in 1 John 1:1-4. It is in the devotional life or "quiet time," through exposure to God's word that the believer discovers on a personal level who God is and what God's will is.

Given the vital importance of the quiet time in the life of the Christian, one would expect that the vast majority of believers would be experiencing exciting times with the Lord through His word. Yet this is simply not the case. Most would admit that their quiet times are not what they should be.

Why is this so? There are basically two reasons. The first is a matter of commitment, the second is a matter of procedure. The first is an issue of the will which the believer must settle while the second is a matter of finding a method that works.

A Matter of Commitment

Do you realize that the only thing preventing you from having an effective quiet time may be you? That's right—you. Do you believe that meeting with the Lord in His word should be the most important activity of your day? Whether we like it or not, the way we spend our time is the best measure of our priorities. If we have time for our job, time for our family, time for hobbies but no time for the Lord we must seriously question whether our job, family, or hobbies are more important than the Lord.

If we love the Lord the way He commands us to in Matthew 22:35-38, with all our heart, soul, and mind, then we will make time to spend with Him, to get to know Him. So the first step in having an effective quiet time is to determine to make fellowship with the Lord *THE* priority of our lives. Then we will set aside time to spend with Him. What kind of time? The amount of time is not the issue. It is the quality of time which is important. It should be regular (Daniel 6:10) and it should be unhurried and uninterrupted (Mark 1:35).

If you are willing to make a commitment of your time on a daily basis for seeking the Lord, you are ninety percent of the way to having an effective quiet time. All that remains is to find a method that will work. This is the easy part!

A Matter of Procedure

You really don't need to be very technical or elaborate. You don't need a divinity degree. All you need is the Bible, a pencil, some paper, some time, and your attention. Why paper and pencil, you may wonder? You will be amazed at how often God instructs you or reveals Himself to you only after you have summarized a passage or recorded its meaning or tried to apply it personally to your own life. It will also be a great delight to have a *written* record of your fellowship with God. Did it ever occur to you that we wouldn't have the Bible as we know it if faithful men had not recorded God's message (see Daniel 7:1)?

These eight steps will help you as you seek the Lord through His word:

1. Pray. Ask God to prepare your heart for His message, to reveal Himself to you, and to show you what He wants to do in your life (see Colossians 1:9,10).

2. Read-Meditate. Read the passage (a verse or paragraph) several times. Meditate on the meaning of the passage. What does it mean? Why is it important?

3. Look-Examine. Carefully examine the passage. Look for names, phrases or instructions that are significant. Notice details, repetition, contrasts, and similarities.

4. Title. Give the passage a short title that reflects its content. This will be helpful in recalling the location of key passages.

5. Date. Record the date of your study. This will be helpful in seeing God's instruction in your life over a period of months and years.

6. Paraphrase-Summarize. Write out the key verse(s) or record a brief paraphrase or summary of the passage. When you can rephrase a passage in your own words, you probably understand it. You will find as you record your summaries, over and over, God will focus your attention on some point that you otherwise would have missed.

7. Apply. Make at least one personal application of the passage. God will provide these if you are open to His leading. Record the application and consider how it can be worked into your life.

8. Pray. Thank God for instructing you. Speak to Him about the application He has given you. Ask Him to work it out in your experience.

If you will get out a blank sheet of paper and begin to follow this little procedure on a consistent basis, you will be amazed at the things God will teach you. I have been using this approach for over 25 years and I am continually overwhelmed at what God is revealing to me about Himself and His will for my life. In Psalm 32:2 the Lord says, "I will instruct you and teach you in the way which you should go; I will counsel you with My eye upon you." It is almost as though God was looking at me as He was causing His word to be written, writing it specifically for my situation, needs, and circumstances.

One question which people often ask is where to start and how much to read. If you are just beginning, I would suggest the Gospel of John as a good place to start. I usually take a paragraph—designated differently in different translations. In the New American Standard Version paragraphs are set off by bold verse numbers; the New Living Translation, the New International Version, and the New King James Version all have paragraph sub-headings. So pick a book and start focusing on the first paragraph following the procedure outlined above. I think working through a book is probably a better approach than skipping around, but the important thing is to be in God's word on a consistent basis.

Many years ago on a visit with us my father asked me what I was studying in my quiet times. When I replied that I was in Luke's Gospel, he said, "Last time I asked you, you were in Luke and that was a couple of months ago." I replied, "Dad, my purpose in my devotions is to meet with God and to hear what He has to say to me, not to see how quickly I can read through a particular book or passage." And that should be your purpose as well.

Reprinted with permission from: Joseph McRae Mellichamp, "Proper Commitment to Priorities and Practical Methods Can Lead to a More Fulfilling Devotional Life," *The Real Issue* [A publication of Christian Leadership Ministries, the faculty ministry of Campus Crusade for Christ], Volume 3, Number 1, 1983.

APPENDIX 2
Reading through the Bible

One of the most rewarding activities I have ever undertaken is reading the Bible through from Genesis to Revelation in a calendar year—from January 1 to December 31. I suspect that most Christians at one time or another have thought about reading through the Bible. But this sounds like a huge undertaking, one that would involve a large time commitment. Especially if it is done in addition to having a daily devotional time as I have outlined in Appendix 1, which should be one's top priority as far as getting into God's Word is concerned. Would you believe that you can read the Bible, Genesis to Revelation, in as little as 15 to 20 additional minutes a day? Most of us spend this much time daily on things which are really not that important, so except for a very few really effective individuals, this would not be a large time burden at all.

Several years ago, I decided to read through the Bible as a New Year's Resolution. One of my motivations for wanting to do this was fear. Let me explain with a story. Years ago, Madeline Murray O'Hare, the famous atheist, was invited to the university at which I taught to debate some of the Christians there. She dispatched one young student who is still a very good friend of mine with one simple question. "Why you little whipper-snapper [or words to this affect], I'll bet you couldn't even name the twelve disciples!" Of course he couldn't. Who could in front of two thousand people? After making several abortive attempts, he admitted that he could not. This was not really a big blunder on his part. But the damage was done, she completely destroyed his credibility. No one in the audience heard another word my friend said that night. As a Christian speaker on university campuses, I am sometimes challenged by individuals and I could imagine someone asking, "Professor Mellichamp, have you ever even read the Bible?" And, of course, I would have had to answer, "No." And that would have been the end of that. So I determined to bite the bullet and do the job, not fully appreciating the wonderful discipline that this would turn out to be.

So I put together a little EXCEL spreadsheet to guide my reading, an average of 85 verses a day from Genesis through Revelation. When I completed the spreadsheet, I decided to share it with some friends in our home fellowship at church and then with all of the staff who are involved with our ministry. Charlie Mack, our representative at Michigan State

University, emailed back to say that he had been challenged by his high school football coach to read through the Bible and that he had done so every year for the last twenty-five years. He went on to say that his inspiration for this was his grandmother who died a few years ago; at her death she had read the Bible from cover to cover every year for 73 years! Wow! I expect Charlie's grandmother is teaching Bible now in heaven— perhaps remedial classes to those who show up without proper preparation.

Charlie's response prompted me to determine to make this an annual goal for as long as I am able. On December 31, 2005, my wife and I both finished reading the Bible from cover to cover for the eighth consecutive year and we are well into the Old Testament for this ninth reading. I have been blessed so much by this discipline, that I am challenging anyone who will listen, to join us. Many of our friends finished reading the Book last year—some for the first or second time, others for the fifth or sixth or seventh time. And now I am challenging you to join us as well. What could be more exciting than reading the story of the greatest person of history? If you want to come along, you will find my EXCEL file at www.facultylinc.com (click on Monday Ministry Minutes in the left side bar and then on #13 from 2005-06). Make as many copies as you need for family and friends. If we are well into the year when you read this and decide to go for it, simply start out on whatever date is convenient and start over again on New Year's Day—you are definitely going to want to continue this once you develop the habit.